1319 Third St SE
New Philadelphia, OH
44663

**KAYAKS
TO
HELL**

KAYAKS
TO
HELL
by William Nealy

Menasha Ridge Press

Hillsborough, North Carolina

Menasha Ridge Press
Route 3 Box 58-G
Hillsborough, North Carolina 27278

Copyright 1982 by William J. Nealy
All rights reserved
Printed in the United States of America
Published by Menasha Ridge Press
Hillsborough, North Carolina 27278

ISBN 0-89732-010-7

Library of Congress Cataloging in Publication Data

Nealy, William, 1953-
   Kayaks to hell.

   Includes index.
   1. White-water canoeing--Comic books, strips, etc.
I. Title.
PN6727.N4K3 1982   741.5'973   82-14247

Acknowledgements

Thanks to Bob Sehlinger, Jeff & Lani Cartier, Henry & Donna Unger, David Vernon, Kathy Cook, Larry Nahmias, Holly "After-all-I-did-edit-your-book-_too_" Wallace, John Barber and all trout everywhere.

Leopards break into the temple and drink to the dregs what is in the sacrificial pitchers; this is repeated over and over again; finally it can be calculated in advance, and it becomes part of the ceremony.

Franz Kafka

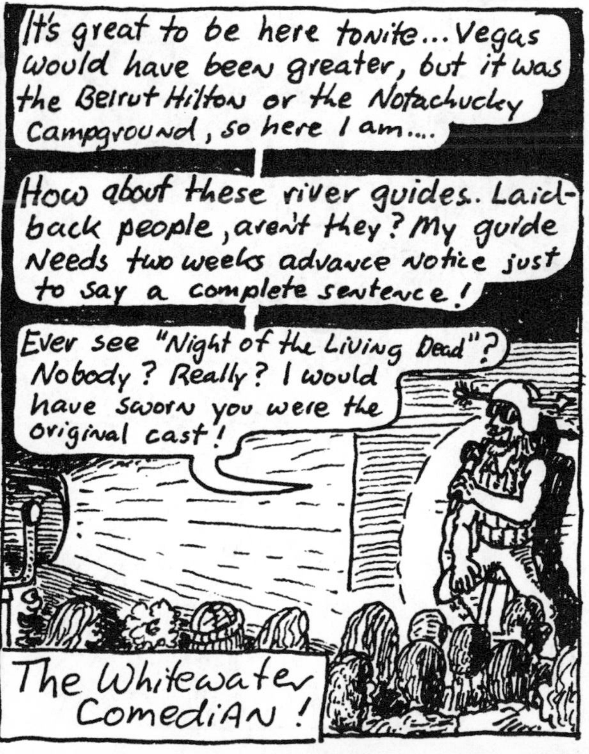
It's great to be here tonite... Vegas would have been greater, but it was the Beirut Hilton or the Notachucky campground, so here I am....
How about these river guides. Laid-back people, aren't they? My guide needs two weeks advance notice just to say a complete sentence!
Ever see "Night of the Living Dead"? Nobody? Really? I would have sworn you were the original cast!
The Whitewater Comedian!

Wasn't dinner terrible—I think the cook got his on-the-job training at Auschwitz!
Have you seen any mountain people yet? Some of 'em look like they grew up in a petri dish, don't they?
How many of you saw "Deliverance"? Wasn't Burt Reynolds fantastic!
Hey! What's the difference between a 'possum and a canoeist?
You can't make a 'possum go "Weeee! Weeee!" while you sodomize it.
Thank you... Thank you very much!
SPLAT

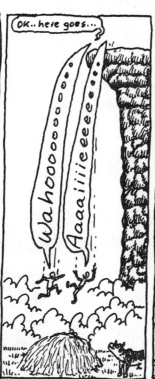

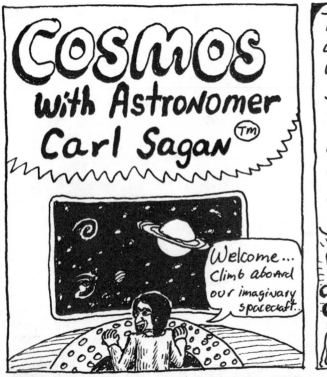

This evening, Cosmos will be examining the principle of Entropy - the universal tendency of all systems, large and small, to fall into total disorder. We have traveled to the mountains of North Carolina, created millions and millions of years ago when the European plate collided with the North American plate... but that's another story and an entirely different discipline.... Assisting us in our demonstration of Entropy will be a river runner who appears to have had considerable experience with entropy already... Let's begin the experiment.
Hi Everybody!
The Following Week...

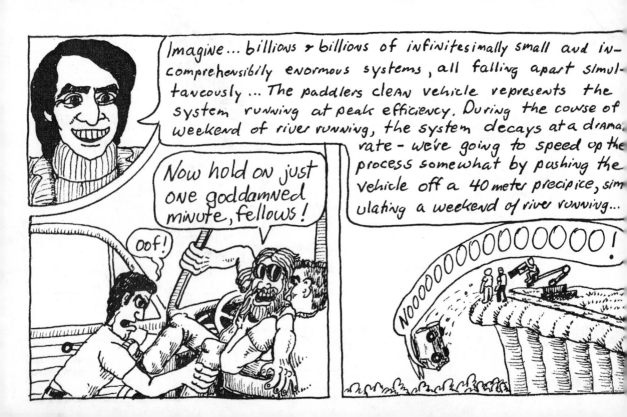

In the 19th century an early pioneer of mechanical physics and astronomy discovered a peculiar attribute of objects in motion. Christian Doppler found that objects moving toward or away from an observer showed a physical shift in the spectra of light and sound. The Doppler Effect, as it is known today is a cornerstone of modern physics and astronomy. We can repeat Doppler's original and elegant experiment demonstrating this phenomenon.

Our next experiment takes us to the mountains of West Virginia, to a bridge high above the New River. Perched over 870 feet above the river, this single span arch bridge should provide an excellent living-laboratory for a demonstration of Kinetic Energy. As you may recall Kinetic Energy of any object is equal to mass times velocity squared times .5. As you can see, the Kinetic energy of an object increases exponentially...

...as velocity increases. We will observe vehicles passing over the bridge and, hopefully, capture high-speed film footage of an object being thrown off the bridge

That projectile packed quite a wallop, didn't it? Notice the compaction of the projectile, compaction that injected 12 ounces of warm beer directly into his brain. It is truly Amazing that this safety helmet, made of a miracle space-age aramid fiber developed in our space program, was positively ineffectual against the 960 foot pounds of kinetic energy. Imagine the awesome power of a comet weighing millions and millions of tons, moving at thousands of miles per second, slamming into the sun. As astounding as this may sound, a comet actually impacted our sun less than a year ago. Photographed by a

The End

Canoeing Businessmen

How to pick up a river person..
Hey.. weren't we in the same affinity group at the Diablo Canyon Nuke Rally?
Lines that frequently work...
① "Great ender - I wish I could do that."
② "Hey babe, ever paddle tandem canoe in Class IV water? Want to?"
③ "I simply love the new North Face dome tents... So aesthetic... beautiful lines... structurally unsurpassed! Oh.. You have one..."
④ "Want to run Big Laurel tomorrow? Small group... maybe just you and me ... You can handle it, NO PROBLEM! I hate big groups..."
⑤ "I have a gas credit card...."

⑥ "It's really wonderful to talk to someone who doesn't have to talk about whitewater all the time".

⑦ "I _hate_ these crowded campgrounds. So noisy.. so impersonal... There's a nice campsite down by the creek that's .... quieter."

⑧ "I see what you're saying... the post impressionist painters were exploring the dialectic of objects and time in totally non-spatial relationships. Wow, that's facinating!"

⑨ Oooh! I'd _love_ to see your slides of the Grand — I'll bet that was incredible! Now? Great!"

How NOT to pick up a river person

① "I don't give backrubs. Ever! "

② "I found the Lord this spring!"

③ "Can't you talk about anything except boats? Boats are _so_ boring!"

④ "They weren't really warts... it went away the next day.... honest! "

General Put-off Approaches..

① Talk about El Salvador.

② Play the Sex Pistols LOUD on the way to the campground.

③ Throw up in his/her car.

④ Talk incessantly about your boyfriend /girlfriend / husband / wife / housemate.

Owed to B. Kliban

River Accessories
from
S & M River
Tours & Supplies . . .

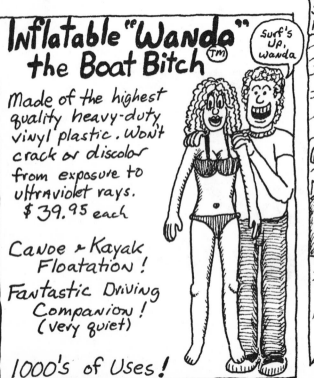

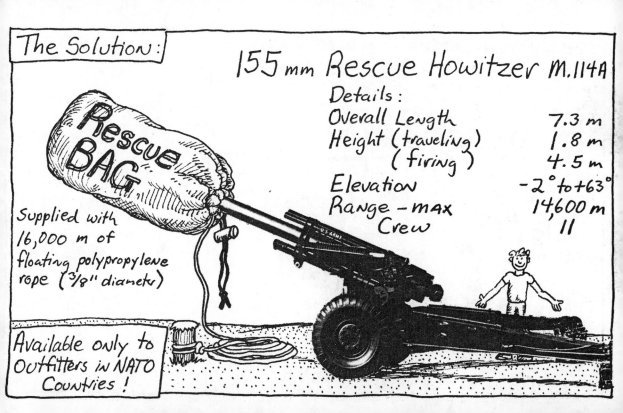

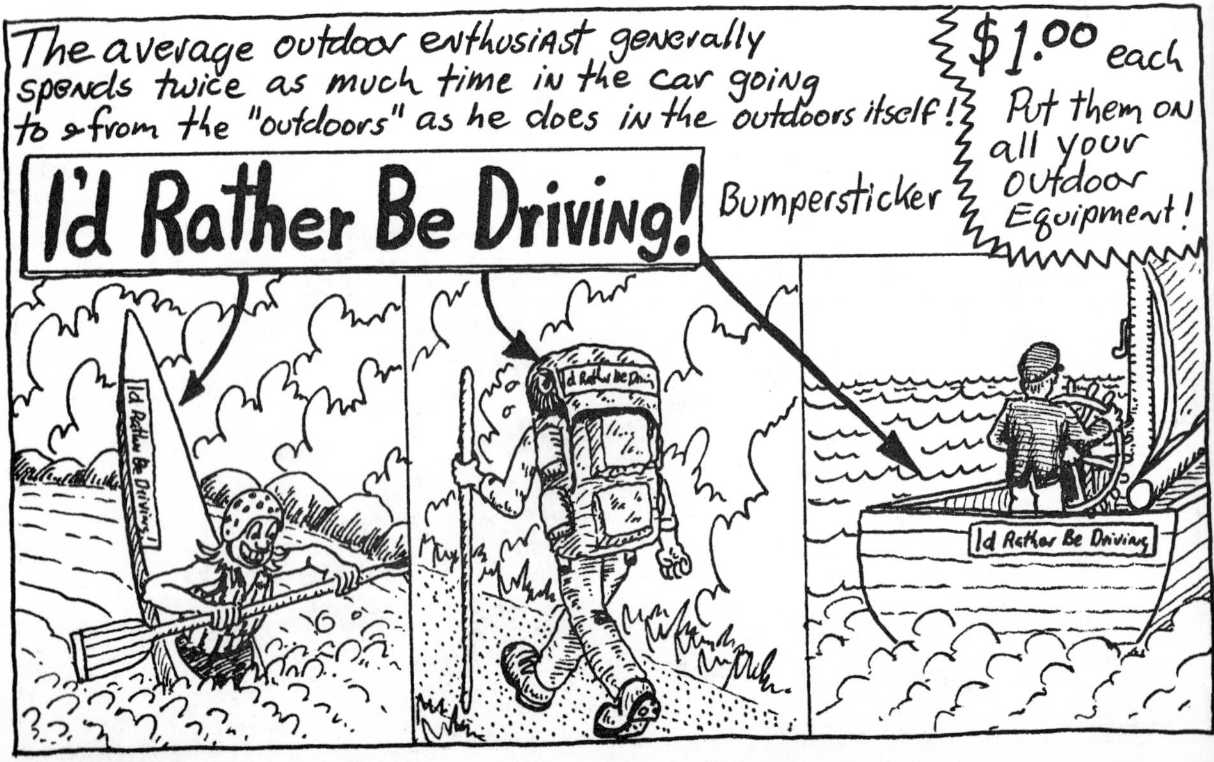
The average outdoor enthusiast generally spends twice as much time in the car going to & from the "outdoors" as he does in the outdoors itself!
$1.00 each
Put them on all your outdoor Equipment!
I'd Rather Be Driving!
Bumpersticker
Id Rather Be Driving!
Id Rather Be Driving
Id Rather Be Driving

Wow! Where'd you get that boat mural?
I've always LOVED Picasso..
Guernica is Soooo wonderful!
You like it?
REALLY.
Get a set of Boat Murals TM for each of your boats! Great icebreaker on the river. For the truly erudite paddler. Full color reproduction printed on waterproof self-sticking vinyl – It'll outlast the boat!
"Guernica" - Pablo Picasso (bow & stern) 19.95
"The Last Supper" - da Vinci (bow & stern)... 24.95
"The Scream" - Munch (Put this one on the bottom of your boat for a real "scream" when you roll!!) 11.95

The Gilley's Whitewater Simulator...
Yahoo!
Ride 'em Cowboy
Go For It!
Only $1685.50 -Installed-
RIDE Boy Ride!
Perfect for Whitewater Clubs and Outfitters !!!!!!!!!!!!!
Patent Pending
Fully Adjustable H_2O

Over the last few years we at S&M River Tours have noticed a strange phenomenon... The very trips that the outfitter thinks will result in dissatisfied customers or (Heaven Forbid!) lawsuits are the very trips the customers loved best!

Broken legs, hypothermia, heat stroke, disease, Abusive or violent river guides, terrible weather, flooded rivers... They love it! They can't get enough of it! In response to overwhelming demand, S&M River Tours has put together some river trips for those customers who insist on a true wilderness ordeal!

S&M River Tours - 1982 Schedule

Hard-core Rafting Adventures
In the jungles & mountains of New Guinea...

Head-hunters!
Hot Weather!
Abusive Guides!
Disease!
Exotic Food!
Fear!

Isn't this Great?

Cold Weather!
Political Repression!
Fierce Rapids!
Forced marches!
Pit Toilets!

Write for Details!

Examination for Whitewater Doctorate—

① Things you can surf: ⓐ Rock, ⓑ Tree ⓒ Wave, ⓓ Cat

② The correct spelling of "Nantahala" is: ⓐ "Nantehila" ⓑ "Nontahula" ⓒ "Nantahala" ⓓ "Nannyheela"

③ [Fill in the blank] A kayak paddle has _____ blades— ⓐ three ⓑ One ⓒ two ⓓ large curved...

④ The distinguishing characteristic of a Class three rapid is: ⓐ Trees ⓑ Anaphylactic Shock ⓒ maneuvering is necessary ⓓ The Treaty of Ghent

⑤ "It is impossible for a person of the female persuasion to roll a kayak."

True or False (circle one) T   F

⑥ Thigh straps would most likely be found in a (an)... ⓐ frying pan, ⓑ hamster cage, ⓒ decked canoe, ⓓ egg

⑦ Synonym for "throw rope"— ⓐ thingie ⓑ Compound fracture, ⓒ rapid floss ⓓ Alexander Haig

⑧ If six boaters run Iron Ring and only four survive, how many boaters didn't make it? ⓐ 0, ⓑ 1, ⓒ 2, ⓓ All of the above

⑨ If you have an ice chest containing a case of beer and a bag of ice, how long will the ice last with an ambient temperature of 90°F.?

A) I hour B) 6 hours C) It doesn't make any difference D) 8 hours

Which of the following was NOT a famous whitewater boater?
A) Walt Blackadar B) John Wesley Powell C) Truman Capote D) William Nealy

Calculate the chances of a successful inner tube run on the Gauley at 7,500 c.f.s. - A) 50% B) 10% C) 0% D) 80%

Means the front of the boat. A) snout B) bumper C) bow D) dingus

Stop!

Correct Answers - ①c, ②c, ③c, ④c ⑤False (stupid!) ⑥c, ⑦c, ⑧c, ⑨c, ⑩c, ⑪c, ⑫c

If you answered move than 60% of the questions correctly, you are now an Expert Boater. Raise your right hand and state;
"I Never come out of my boat."
Congratulations!
You may sign your card.
cut along dotted line

Tiny black frames Available !

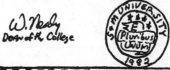

S&M University of Whitewater Sciences
Chapel Hill, North Carolina

KNOW All Men By These Presents That Upon This Date, S&M University Has Conferred Upon

the Degree of
Doctor of Whitewater Science

W. Nealy
Dean of the College

Willie Nealy
President

E Pluribus Unum
S&M UNIVERSITY
1982

Another Paddling Trip. . . .

Well a'him proud to be an okie from Muskogee..
restrooms
Kittys
Tom Cats
We're dead
Ulp!
This boy who sold my kid that LSD paddled a boat just like that....
Oh my God...
Tee hee
You betcha Jim-Bob!
Hey Ed... Play that'un about th' Faggot Trucker!
Har Har Har

..but suppose you could travel at light speed and you fired a death ray at an alien traveling toward you at light speed... how fast would the death ray be going?
What is that howling noise? Damn tape player...
But you can't exceed the speed of light— It's like the universal speed limit
Oh shit... a cop!
Weeooowe ooowee ooo weeooowe ooo weeoo
It's supposed to be an immutable cosmic law.. at least according to Einstein!

Hey man! Why we stopping?
godogodogodogodogodogodogodogodogodogodogodogodogodogod
He's gonna know I'm stoned.. Gotta concentrate... "good evening officer. What's the problem?" "Good evening officer, What's the problem".. "Good evening offi..."
Oh God! My head is shrinking
Well I met her in a honky tonk in memphis...

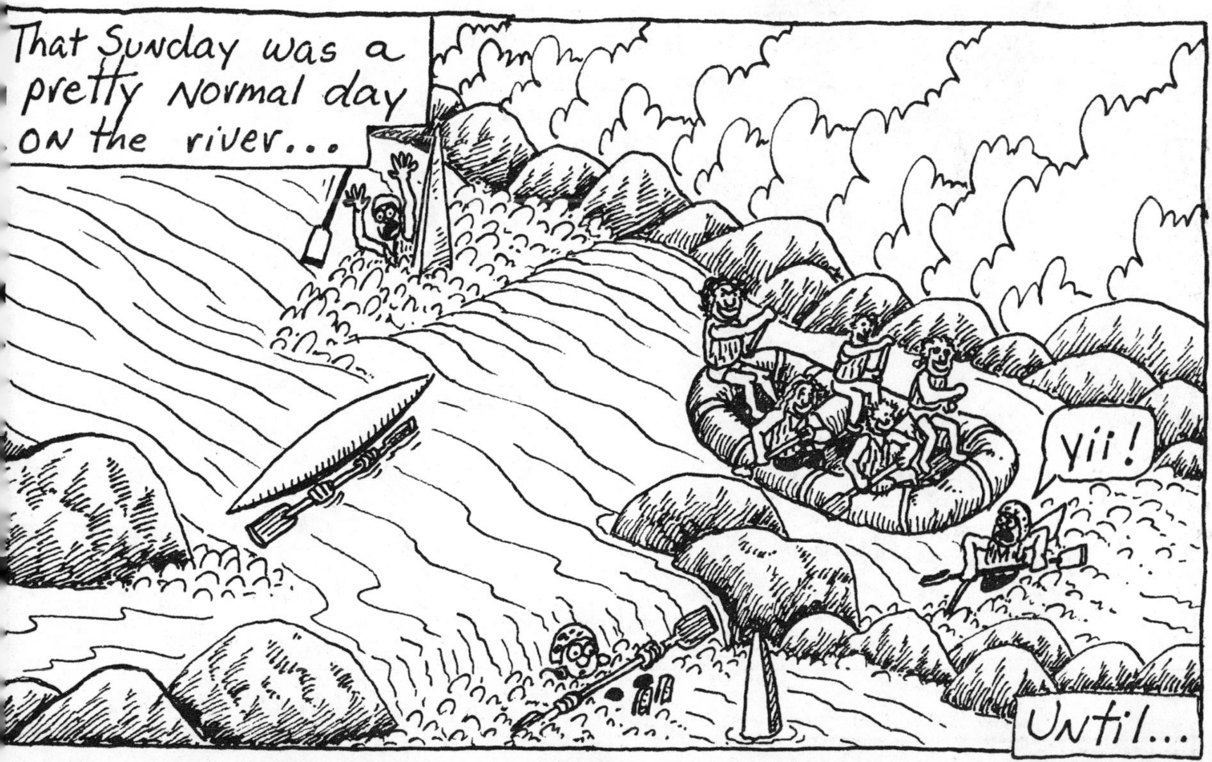
That Sunday was a pretty Normal day on the river...
yii!
Until...

Good Lord! Are you OK? Some lunatic musta dropped something off the bridge...
Oh NO!
Suuurrree... Immm fiiiinnnneee.....
...beeeeeerr caaan Iii thiiinnk....

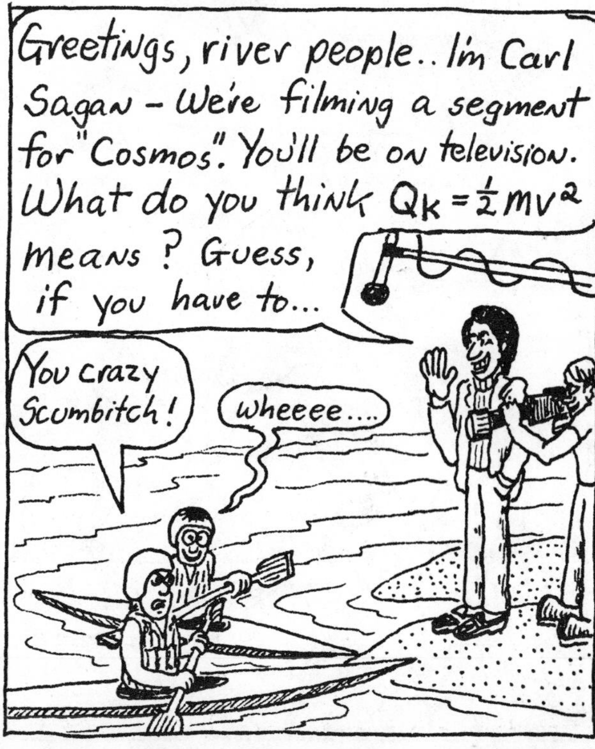
Greetings, river people.. I'm Carl Sagan - We're filming a segment for "Cosmos". You'll be on television. What do you think $Q_K = \frac{1}{2}mv^2$ means? Guess, if you have to...
You crazy Scumbitch!
wheeee....

Where have you guys been! We won't be able to get back until three o'clock in the morn.. JEEEZ! What happened to him!?!
We met Carl Sagan! It was GREAT!
Carl Sagan did THAT!
Naw! You don't understand. I'm gonna be on TV!
mumble mumble

...and he wants to read my river journals... start a correspondence!
Sure man, right!
I mean, this guy's brilliant!
Maybe we ought to go to "Mars" again, eh?
Forget "Mars", guys.. Ya'll are weird enough already!
Unbelievable!
mumble mumble
mumble mumble
mumble mumble.....

Before | After

Why Klansmen Wear Hoods...

Kayaking on Fantasy Island..

HMS TITANIC

...miraculously they survived a mid-Atlantic collision with a gigantic iceberg. Had the Titanic not been carrying a cargo of experimental industrial tape it is believed that all hands could have been lost!

It is NOT KNOWN exactly who invented Duct Tape but who-ever it was... We salute you!

Pssst- hey kid... Valium... speed... acid... placidyl... coke.... lomotil...

Help! Help!

DUCT TAPE

The DuctTape Monument

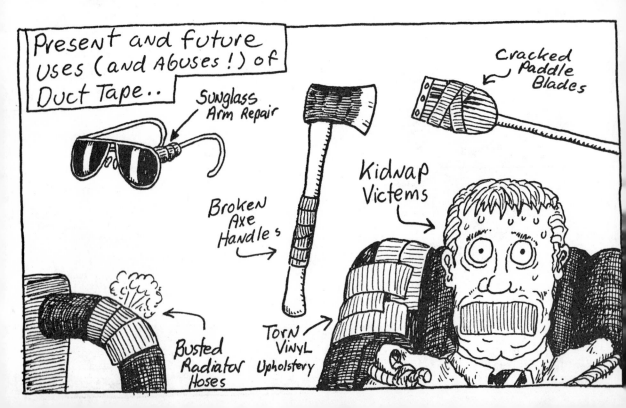

..One Giant Leap for Mankind..
RRRIIIPP!
Whoops...
Commander Armstrong.. This is mission Control- Quick! The Duct Tape!
Frequently its use has been hidden from the American Public!

Duct tape has been used for years by British rockclimbers to secure chocks in shallow cracks and rugosities..
Go for it, Mate!

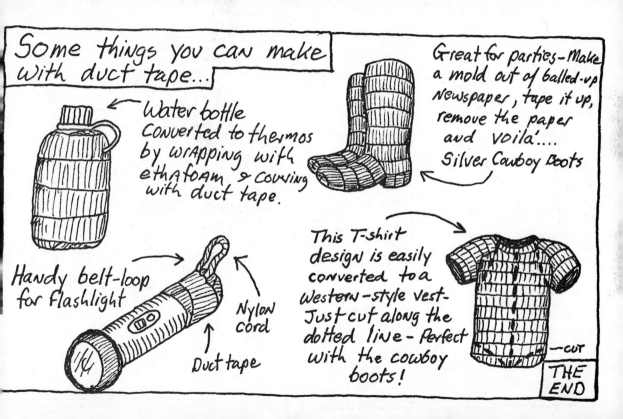

A Cunning Array of stunts

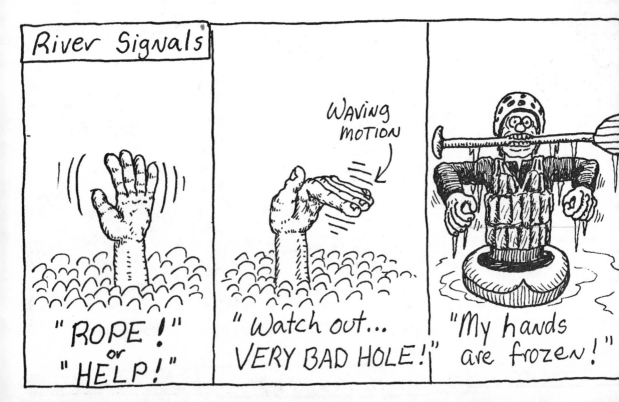

"Go Away!"
or
"Get your boat off my boat!"

"Aarrgh!"
or
"Perhaps my thigh straps are too tight."

"Those rafters are in serious trouble..."
or
"I've got a date with the raft guide"

How to tell the difference between an alien and a trout fisherman...

Alien (left panel):
- Antennae
- Three fingers
- Ray Gun

Trout Fisherman (right panel):
- Baseball Cap
- Fly Rod
- Net
- Inner Tube
- Waders

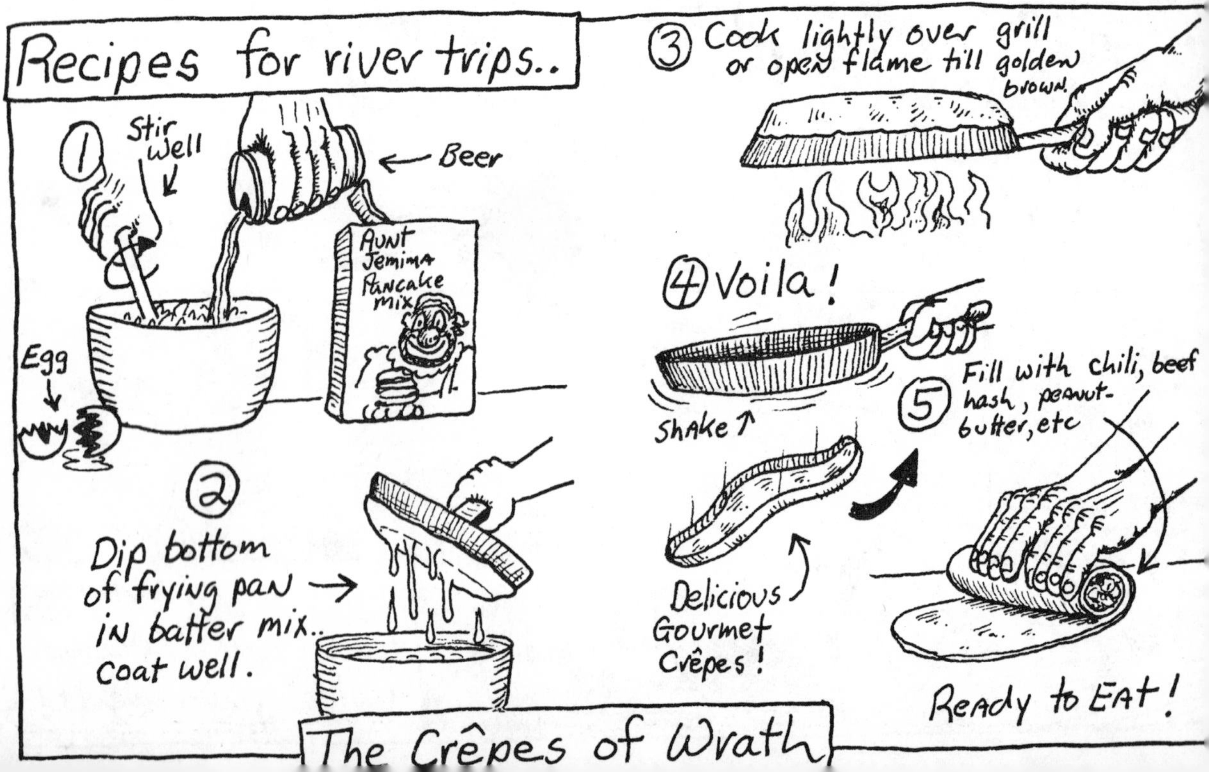

Recipes for river trips..

① Stir well

Egg

Beer

Aunt Jemima Pancake Mix

② Dip bottom of frying pan in batter mix.. coat well.

③ Cook lightly over grill or open flame till golden brown

④ Voila!

Shake ↑

Delicious Gourmet Crêpes!

⑤ Fill with chili, beef hash, peanut-butter, etc

Ready to EAT!

The Crêpes of Wrath

Aspirin Sandwich

Always serve with cold beer and alka seltzer

Aspirin

Great for saturday breakfast or Sunday Brunch....

Many people think of aspirin only as a drug. It's a tasty food too. Besides relieving pain, aspirin is a Nutritious source of salicylic acid which aids the body's ability to regenerate dead or damaged braincells.

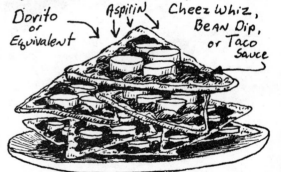

Dorito or Equivalent

Aspirin

Cheez Whiz, Bean Dip, or Taco Sauce

A taste of old Mexico!

Aspirin hors d'oeuvres

Soup

There is nothing quite like a sierra cup full of HOT soup after a day of serious paddling.

You'll need:
Meat (optional),
Vegetables (optional)
Salt,
pepper,
and a can
or two of
whatever is
lying around
(optional),
+Water.

Heh heh...

Remember - "A soup boiled is a soup spoiled"

Beer → for the chef!

STEW

Basically the same recipe as "soup" only you cook it longer and use less water. Add flour to thicken, as necessary.

Road-kill Stew - suitable for rabbit, squirrel, opossum, etc. Cut up and parboil meat - Add to vegetables, etc. - Cover with water and simmer in large pot for several hours until all ingredients are tender. Stew is always better the next day.

Oh god!

Caution! Box turtles are NOT suitable for road stew! They eat mushrooms that contain toxins harmful to humans!!

Damn! Oh well - beats Doritos for dinner

BLAM

The Essentials, please...

Peanut Butter & Jelly — Cheap, foolproof.....No refrigeration required. The perfect food! If you run out of bread, don't panic — This stuff is good on anything you can smear it on!

Potatoes — The only good kind of tuber, potatoes can be fried, baked, boiled, mashed, steamed, etc. ad infinitum. Potatoes need no refrigeration, they're nutritious and practically anyone with an I.Q. above 40 can cook them. Also great for throwing at road signs and other boater's cars.

ONIONS — Maintenance free and good cooked or raw. Onions go with any recipe (except maybe apple cobbler!). Make sure your "tent-mate" eats some too.

great @ peanut butter!

BANANAS — Excellent eating anytime. Batter & fry up for a unique culinary experience. Warning — If one of these babies gets squashed in your down bag...!!Carimba!! What a mess!

Beer & Wine — Drink it while you cook...pour it in the stew.... marinate stuff in it..... You name it! If the food turns out bad, so what! Have another beer.. no prob.

Helpful Hints—

An old workglove makes pot clamps obsolete — Also good for pulling baked potatoes out of the coals.

Stick — Handy for poking around in the fire. Also perfect for pounding on sideline chefs and people who walk up and say...

"Ugh — What's _THAT_?"

Dogs are useful for wiping greasy hands on. They are also quite adept at pre-cleaning dirty pots & pans. These self-contained garbage disposals are cheap and easy to maintain. Koreans like them boiled or fried!

Gas — white or auto-dangerous to transport and use but what the hell. Gas (a.k.a. "hamburger helper") is the only way to ignite wet wood. Good luck.

Ice Chest — don't scrimp, get a good big one that two people can sit on w/o breaking. Try to buy food that doesn't require refrigeration so the beer & wine isn't too crowded. Keep ice well-drained and it will last longer.

The Missing Link

Introduction to "C-boats; can't stay in 'em, can't live without 'em!" —

During my river travels over the past year, lots of disgruntled C-boaters have approached me and "suggested" that perhaps I should actually TRY a C-boat before casting stones at C-boaters in general. I rarely throw rocks at C-boats and IF I do, it's at a particular one, not some general entity... REALLY!

OK guys, you win. I paddle one now (I'd be in it right now but "they" are making me write this!). My knees throb when the barometer drops... I can no longer walk unassisted at the take out. My ankles look like warthogs and I've got permanent cockpit creases on each hip. My elbows are hopelessly scarred. The condition of my hands is best left unsaid. My boat leaks like a WhiteHouse aide. I hate my bracing system. My paddle got terminally crunched yesterday... along with my shoulder. I talk endlessly about C-boats & "canoeing". I have joined the ranks of the living dead. I hope everyone is happy now. Never has a greater price been paid for objectivity!

[To my kayaking buddies: Don't worry — I haven't sold my kayak. I'm keeping it around for when the river floods and I totally wimp out. Sorry guys.]

C-Boater's Pain Scale

Zone 1 – Usually begins minutes after putting in. Mild foot cramps and a dull throbbing in the ankles and toes.

Zone 2 – Characterized by a mild respite from the initial wave of Z-1 pain followed by a rapid onset of Z-1 symptoms that get progressively worse very quickly!

Zone 3 – Recognized by the beginning of knee pain coupled with intense shooting pain in the ankles.
Note: Kayakers never go beyond Zone 3

Zone 4 – Pain preceded by a numbness & tingling similar to having your foot go to sleep. A good time to get out of the boat and do jumping jacks on the nearest rock.

Zone 5 – Terrible pain: The main way to ascertain if you're in Zone 5 is if the pain does not go away after being out of the boat for 3 minutes or more.

Zone 6 – Hideous Pain – If you get out of your boat you either (A) crawl around & moan, or (B) walk like the hunchback of Notre Dame.
Note – few open boaters break this threshold.

Zone 7 – Unbearable pain in the ankles that takes your mind off your knees. Similar to having icepicks jabbed into the top of the foot.

Zone 8 – Unbearable pain in your knees that takes your mind off your ankles. Few other than C-boaters & Italian government officials ever experience this type of pain.

Zone 9 – Indescribable pain that tends to be generalized rather than the specific stab-like pain of zones 7 & 8. Concentrate on the takeout and cold beer.

Zone 10 – Zone 9^3! – Overwhelming pain from the mid-thigh down coupled with high anxiety and an intense desire to leap out of the boat & die quietly.

Postscript to Whitewater Home Companion...

[Gravestones labeled: Pipeline, Finders Keepers, S-turn Rapid, Smooth Ledge]

Another Corps Coup!

It saddens me to report the untimely demise of several intimate acquaintances of mine—I refer to the numerous rapids inundated by a lake on the lower Haw River [See _Whitewater Home Companion_ - pp 90, 93-94].

In order to obey the precepts of the Southern Recreational Lake Theorem ["Thou shalt not have to travel further than 50 miles in any direction without encountering a large lake"] the Army Corps has destroyed over half of one of the top whitewater runs in the state of North Carolina. To add insult to injury, its _my_ home river.

In response to the lake we formed a river protection organization to try to force the state political machine to enforce existing state environmental protection regulations protecting the river. While trying to end the legal(!) dumping of thousands of gallons a day(!!) of raw sewage, formaldehyde, textile dyes, heavy metals, petroleum by-products, insecticides, etc. _into_ the river we discovered that the state environmental agency didn't ask what was being dumped, just how much! There isn't even a space on the licensing form to state what is actually being dumped !!! I sincerely hope that Idi Amin and the A.E.C. don't get wind of this pearl of bureaucratic obscurantism or we'll have radioactive corpses floating down the river too...

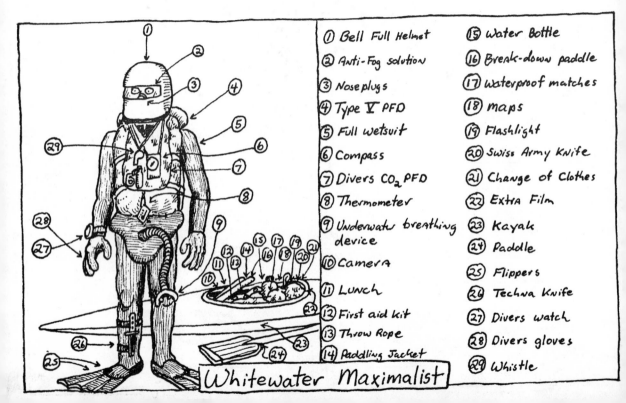

① Bell Full Helmet
② Anti-Fog solution
③ Nose plugs
④ Type V PFD
⑤ Full wetsuit
⑥ Compass
⑦ Divers CO_2 PFD
⑧ Thermometer
⑨ Underwater breathing device
⑩ Camera
⑪ Lunch
⑫ First aid kit
⑬ Throw Rope
⑭ Paddling Jacket
⑮ Water Bottle
⑯ Break-down paddle
⑰ Waterproof matches
⑱ Maps
⑲ Flashlight
⑳ Swiss Army Knife
㉑ Change of Clothes
㉒ Extra Film
㉓ Kayak
㉔ Paddle
㉕ Flippers
㉖ Techna Knife
㉗ Divers watch
㉘ Divers gloves
㉙ Whistle

Whitewater Maximalist

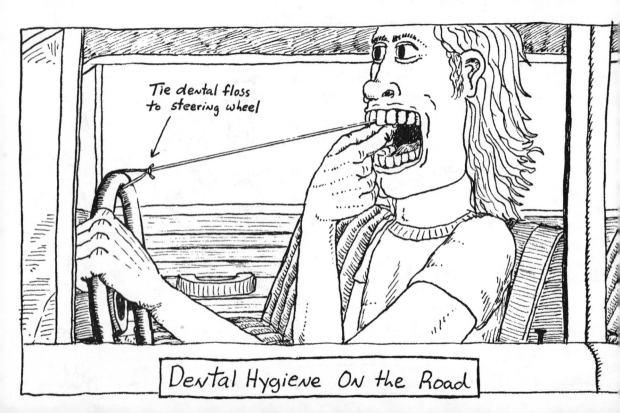

Glossary, slang terms, and terminology

backender – a reverse ender. The boat stands vertically on the stern end instead of the bow end.

bad – good (although sometimes "bad" is bad.

boat scouting – inspecting a rapid from your boat by eddy-hopping and running it in stages.

boulder – extra big rock (refrigerator size and up).

boulder garden – a rapid or shoal ornamented with lots of boulders.

canoe – A.K.A. "open boat." – an elongated symmetrical river craft usually paddled by one or two people using single-bladed paddles. A canoe with a deck is referred to as a "decked canoe".

canoeist— see "C-boater" or "open boater"

C-boat— decked canoe — A.K.A. "pain boat", see "C-boater".

C-boater — Depending on your perspective, C-boaters are either the most highly skilled form of boater or the most highly masochistic. On the river C-boaters look like kayakers with canoe paddles, on shore they are usually limping or completely unable to walk.

cfs — "cubic feet per second" — A.K.A. "cubes" — refers to the volume of water passing an established point of reference on a river.

creek— A.K.A. "run", "crick", — a **diminutive** river.

crunchola - What happens when you hit a rock.

decked canoe - A single-person decked canoe is referred to as a "C-1", a two-person decked canoe is a "C-2".

C-1

WOOSH!

I said "watch out for that rock" Nitwit!

Drop - Any vertical change in the riverbed that is perpendicular. Drops higher than six feet are frequently called "waterfalls".

Dynamic - As in "dynamic peel-out", "dynamic eddy", etc. Used to describe an extreme form of Anything. Dynamic lunch stop ?!

eat it - to flip over or take a nasty swim. Variations include: "chewed," ddy-surfed", "creamed", "crunched", "douched", "eaten", "mangled","mashed, munched", "mutilated", "puréed", "stuffed", "thrashed", "trashed", "woofed",etc.

eddy - The relatively calm spots found on the downstream side of rocks, pilings, etc. Normally eddies are good places to be, but on a floodstage river they can become whirlpools or bizarre boat naps

eddy fence - high water phenomenon usually. The eddy line becomes a violent hole-like mess that can eat boats and swimmers.

Direction of H2O flow →

Rock

Eddy Fence or line

EODY

eddy current

Eddy Fence or Line

eddy line - the interface of the downstream flow and the eddy current. The wet version of wind shear.

ender - Aka "pop up", "endo", - standing the boat on end in holes or on waves. A good ender is when the boat gets stood perpendicula to the river and shot completely out of the water. A great ender is when you and your boat land in a raft. See "backender" and "pirouette".

entrapment - Getting trapped in or out of your boat in moving H₂O. This is generally an ultra-serious life-threatening situation requiring instantaneous rescue. Entrapment is avoided in most cases by always scouting rapids, avoiding blind drops and strainers, and never ever walking and/or dragging your feet in fast-moving water.

Articles on entrapment rescue techniques can be found in the AWA Journal and the River Safety Task Force Newsletter - read them!

Foot Entrapment   Boat Entrapment

Eskimo Roll - A self-rescue technique used by decked (and open!) boaters.

Rolling is done by executing a series of upside-down underwater paddle strokes which, with the correct body-english, usually results in an upright (and happy) boater.

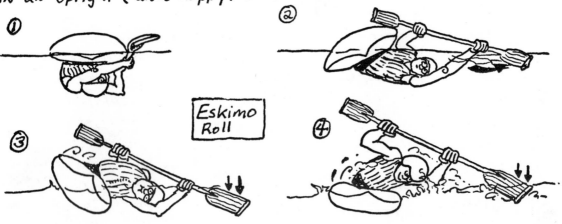

① ② ③ ④

Eskimo Roll

Expert boater - Usually a self-conferred title [see "S&M Products"], the qualifications for "expert" are nebulous and vary regionally. An "expert boater" can be : Any competent boater, Anyone who paddles the Gauley and lives, Anyone who owns or works in a whitewater specialty store, any river guide, any raft guide, any outfitter and/or anyone who makes maps of rivers or writes river guidebooks.

Falls - Aka "waterfall" - Any vertical drop higher than six feet.

Flat Water - Any water that is still or flows in a sluggish manner. The bane of whitewater boaters, flat water is actually paddled for "fun" in some parts of the country !?

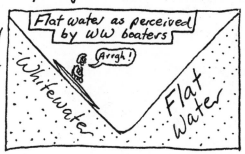

Funny Water - Usually anything but. Funny water is mostly found on high-volume or floodstage rivers and manifests itself as whirlpools percolating eddies, exploding waves, mobile eddy fences, etc.

gradient – Refers to the steepness of the riverbed. Gradient is commonly expressed as the drop in feet-per-mile average.

Hair – A river or creek possessing a combination of high gradient, high volume, and extreme technical difficulty. Hair or "hairy" are also descriptive terms for any rapid, hole, etc. that is profoundly frightening / dangerous.

helmet – Aka. "beanie", "hat", "brain bucket" – rigid head protection device.

hero route – Most difficult imaginable route through a rapid

hole – see "hydraulic"

hot dog – Extraordinarily Acrobatic boater or a beginner with a death wish.

Hydraulic – A.K.A. "hole", "sousehole", "vertical eddy", "keeper", "reversal". Hydraulics are caused by water flowing over an obstacle and creating a recirculating flow. Hydraulics come in an infinite variety and are a source of amusement and/or fear for boaters. A hole used as an eddy is referred to as a "keeper eddy".

Kayak – A.k.a. "yak", "K-1", "river volkswagon" – The most common decked river-craft and the easiest decked boat to master. Kayaks are highly maneuverable, fast, and require a moderate degree of skill to paddle. Most kayakers sit in the boat and use a two-bladed paddle.

Kayak

Kayaker – Anyone who paddles (or attempts to paddle) a kayak. From the point of view of non-paddlers, Kayakers are generally perceived to be @ the whitewater equivalent of Hells Angels, or ⑬ brain-damaged river loonies, or both. Easily recognized on the river, kayakers tend to travel in large groups and engage in bizarre rituals in each and every rapid. Kayakers tend to view all other types of rivercraft as slow-moving obstacles to wave/hole playing, with rafts being most disliked of all. Canoes are tolerated as amusing entertainment and/or comic relief, particularly when a swamping or spill occurs. Decked canoeists [see "C-boater"] seem to be universally disliked and distrusted by kayakers. "Rumbles" between kayakers an C-boaters are not uncommon in the Southeast. Never call a kayaker a "kayakist" or a "feelthy two-blader", at least to his face.

local(s) - Recognized by "Goin' fishin'?" or "What's that, a ski?" and similar questions. Locals are the people indigenous to whatever area you happen to be in. Generally friendly when treated with respect. Locals in mountain areas tend to look upon whitewater boating as an activity somewhere between devil worship and heroin addiction.

lunch bunny - A.K.A. "female raft guide trainee" - Not to be confused with the true woman raft guide, lunch bunnies are hired to provide a little tits & ass for the customers and to assure everybody that, even on the river, a woman's place is in the kitchen.

open boater - A.K.A. "canoeists", "canoers" - Anyone who paddles an open canoe. Easily recognizable for their proclivity for swimming class 4 rapids and thinking it's fun. Often heard saying "shit, that's easy with two blades."

peelout - pulling out of an eddy pointed upstream. When you cross the eddy line the downstream current snatches the bow of the boat and spins the boat abruptly 180° and you're facing downstream - that is unless you forgot to lean downstream - say "hi!" to the trout.

pillow – a cushion of water on the upstream face of a rock or boulder. Can be braced into in tight situations.

pin – see "entrapment"

pirouette – An ender with a half-twist... You pivot the standing boat with a crossdraw and land facing downstream.

pool – a calm area just below a rapid.

put in – The place where you park the car and get in your boat.

raft – A.k.a. "rubber bus", "pig boat", "barge" etc. An inflatable rubber boat used mainly by commercial outfitters. The one good thing about a raft is the vast quantity of beer and food it can carry.

raft guide – aka. "guide", "boatman" – the man or woman in charge of the raft. Raft guides typically come in two varieties – the jocks and the crazies. They can also be classified by region – West of the Mississippi you find the Western Boat Toad and, naturally, in the East you find the Eastern Boat Toad. Fun people, mostly.

rafters – a.k.a. "breeders", "customers" etc. [see "turkey"] Rafters are typically middle-class Caucasian professionals who think whitewater was designed and built by Walt Disney. Life is one big E-ride... wa-hoo! Often resented by private boaters, rafters do provide some of us with occasional free lunches, money, and some great cartoon material.

rapid – a section of river characterized by increased gradient, fast water, waves and/or holes, rocks, and assorted other obstacles. There is a controversy in the higher echelons of the W.W. community regarding the use of "rapid" as opposed to "rapids". The plurality advocates insist that the singular form "rapid" isn't even found in the dic-

tionary! Sorry guys —"Rapid" singular is right there under "R" in both Webster
and the Oxford English Dictionary.

river left - on the left facing downstream. Since most all rivers flow
in only one direction, the downstream orientation eliminates lots
of confusion. see "river right".

river right - on the right facing downstream.

rock garden - a rapid or shoal ornamented with numerous rocks.

roll - a small loaf of bread, usually baked - Similar to a muffin or
biscuit.

roostertail - A fountain-like liquid obstacle caused by fast-moving
water striking a rock and spewing in an upwardly direction

safety rope - A.k.a. "throw rope", "rescue rope", "rapid floss" - An essential piece of river running equipment, safety rope(s) should accompany any group down any river! Also great for impromtu boat-thief lynchings!

Scouting - to visually inspect a rapid, drop, etc. from the shore.

shoal - a nebulous term referring to anything from a rock garden to a gravel bar. Usually a shallow ledgy section with fast water and lots of obstacles to hang up on.

shuttle - What you do before and after the river trip. This involves putting some type of vehicle at the takeout so you can retrieve the vehicle you left at the put in.

Shuttle bunny - Somebody's girlfriend or wife who runs the shuttle and waits while you have fun on the river. It goes like this: "Darling,

maybe I'd better paddle solo today – this is a really tough river...."
Poof! Instant shuttle bunny.

slide show – common weekend ritual for paddlers with nowhere to go. For females and non-paddlers, the normal whitewater slide show is roughly equivalent to an overdose of Valium or Thorazine.

sneak – to take the easiest (or safest) route thru a rapid. Can also mean to covertly portage a rapid. A.K.A. "chicken route", "tourist route," "girl scout route". See "hero route".

speared – A.K.A. "harpooned" – Being speared is getting stabbed by either the bow or stern of a decked boat. Commonly occurring in eddies and on surfing waves, getting speared is roughly the equivalent of being run over by a U.P.S. truck.

stopper – Either a hole or breaking wave that stops you dead.

strainer – Any obstacle in the river that allows water to pass through but not boats and people. Fallen trees, wire, fence, debris, etc. can be extremely dangerous and should always be given a wide berth whenever possible.

surf – to ride a wave on its upstream face or to play in a hole (intentionally or unintentionally). Hole surfing is easier than wave surfing because once you get in the hole, it does all the work.

take out – The place where you get out of the boats and into the cars.

tuber – A.K.A. "Hole Bait", "Dead Meat", [see "Turkey"]. A tuber is a root-like vegetable and/or someone who runs rivers in an inner tube, usually without the benefit of helmet, lifejacket, and common sense. Despite the charming egalitarian aspects of the "sport", tubing is proof that natural selection is still at work. The tuber of the future will be scarce but probably quite strong. Improvement in intelligence is not likely.

turkey – [see "rafter", "tuber",] Generic term for novice boaters, rafters, and tubers. To expert boaters it describes everyone else. Variations include: bozo, nebbish, neednoid, pinhead, touroid, yahoo, etc.

tweeze – A.K.A. "Thread the Needle"– to take a tight route through two or more obstacles. Also may mean to catch a tiny seam between two holes.

walk the dog – to portage a rapid, drag your boat, or covertly indulge in controlled substances.

wave – You _know_ what a wave is.

undercut rock – a rock, boulder, or rock formation that has

been eroded just beneath the surface of the water. Undercut can also refer to a submerged overhanging rock. Radical under-cutting can result in a mushroom-like configuration with the base of the "cap" just under the surface. Extremely dangerous for paddlers, undercut rocks are often jammed with logs and other river debris, creating nasty undercut strainers!

Undercut Rock

Undercut strainer

Zoo — A.K.A. "E-ride", "Six Flags Over Neoprene" — Term used to de-scribe any particularly crowded or overcommercialized river or rapid. Examples: Swimmers Rapid-Yok, Ocoee on any summer weekend, New River Gorge between 11:00 Am and 2:00 Pm, etc.

River Maps by William "Not-Bill" Nealy

(1) American River-South Fork-California-1980
  (A) Chili Bar to Camp Lotus
  (B) Camp Lotus to Folsum Lake

(2) Brown's Canyon of the Arkansas-Colorado-1979

(3) Chattahoochee River-Georgia
  (A) Upper Section-1981
  (B) Lower Section (Atlanta)-1982

(4) Chattooga River-N. Georgia
  (A) Section Three-1980
  (B) Section Four-1979

(5) Cheat River Canyon-West Virginia-1981 (Revised 1982)

(6) French Broad & Big Laurel Creek-W. North Carolina-1981

(7) Gauley River-West Virginia-1979

(8) Haw River-North Carolina (Central Piedmont)-1978

(9) Hiwassee River-E. Tennessee-1978

(10) Nantahala River Gorge-North Carolina-1978 (Revised 1981)

(11) New River Gorge-West Virginia-1978

(12) Nolichucky River Gorge-W. North Carolina-1979

(13) Ocoee River-E. Tennessee-1978 (Revised 1982)

(14) Ocoee River-Special Flume Commemorative Map-1982

(15) Shangrilaha-Location Secret-1980

(16) Youghiogheny River ("Lower Yok")-Pennsylvania-1980

(17) National Wild & Scenic Rivers-1981

Available from: Menasha Ridge Press
Route 3 Box 58-G
Hillsborough, NC 27278